17 Ways to Manage Your Reputation Using Social Media

What Are They Saying About You?

17 Ways to Manage Your Reputation Using Social Media

Copyright © 2011 by Michelle Mullen

ISBN 9781466247253

Table of Contents

Introduction

Social media marketing is in, traditional advertising is out.

In the next few years, this might be the scenario in the marketing industry as businesses turn to the Internet—particularly social media—to reach out to their target customers. Statistics show that social media marketing fares better in terms of profit-making than traditional forms of advertising. This fact cannot stress enough how social media has revolutionized the way companies do business these days. Gone are the days when consumers actively look for products and services they need. Taking a 180-degree turn, goods and services are now finding customers through social media.

Nowadays, more and more Internet marketers have realized social media's potential to be a goldmine. Yes, you read it right—there's money in practically every social activity on the Web: blogging, podcasting, sharing content on Facebook, among many others. Many wise marketers out there have been tapping social media tools to their business' advantage.

This book is by no means all encompassing. It does not attempt to create a one-size-fits-all social media marketing campaign for business owners like you. Instead, it presents all the tips and tricks you need to start your own social media strategies. You can use these strategies to devise your own plans and to take advantage of social media's power to establish your brand and reputation in the market. Every business is unique, and so are your needs. This book was written with this fact in mind.

The highlight of this book is a chapter that discusses each of the 17 social media tools that you can use to make your business known to as many people as possible. How do you tweet or blog your way to your success? In addition, the power of social media as it relates to when people search for you in the search engines. Within these pages, you will discover the answer to that and other questions you may have in mind right now.

Ask yourself, "Am I ready to take my business to the next level?" Social media may help you achieve exactly that.

So, let's begin then, shall we?

Chapter 1

Social Media and Your Business Reputation

What is Social Media?

Social media is an encompassing term for websites and online technologies that allow people to easily exchange messages, information, opinions, insights, and resources. It comes in multiple forms: blogs, online forums, photo sharing sites, video sharing sites, social networking sites, social bookmarking sites, presence apps or microblogs, and streaming sites. Majority of the content in social media websites consists of text, images, video, and audio.

HigherResultsMarketing.com

Unlike traditional or offline media, social media empowers individuals by giving them the ability to create and control Internet content. This is in stark contrast to how the traditional media controls and filters the content it delivers to its audience.

Another difference between the two forms of media concerns space and time. Traditional media is constrained by deadlines and the available airtime and print space. On the other hand, social media works real time (meaning the messages become available once they are received) 24 hours a day, 7 days a week.

Social media is measurable while traditional media is not. Companies that use traditional advertising cannot measure the effectiveness of their campaign and customer awareness of their brand until customers purchase the products. In contrast, user responses and actions about a certain brand or product can be easily determined in social media.

Social media has become a hit among people across various age groups simply because it is fun. This media also makes it possible for people to find friends, business contacts and partners, and various communities where they could fit in. TV, newspaper, and other traditional forms of media do not provide what social media can: the opportunity to interact with others.

It is no wonder why businesses take advantage of the interactive nature of social media to promote their brand, engage customers, and establish ties with customers and business partners. Both small and large-scale businesses create their own social media marketing campaigns so that they can get their message across to their target customers.

Why Use Social Media for Your Business?

At this point, you might be asking, "Is using social media worth my time, money, and effort?" Before we get to that, it is worth looking at some of the advantages of harnessing the power of social media for your business.

- **Social media does not cost much.** Perhaps this is the number one reason for the popularity of social media among individuals and businesses. Some tools are even free! You can advertise your brand all you want without investing a huge amount of money, thanks to social media websites.
- **It gives your business a competitive edge.** Take advantage of one social media website or tool every month, and by the end of the year, your business will be ahead of the competition.
- **It serves as a platform for promoting your products or services.** You can also use social media to create a buzz about your products or services, so you can reach a wider customer base.
- **It gives you feedback directly from customers.** You might as well study their behavior and opinions about your business by going to online communities (e.g. forums, blogs, microblogs, etc.) where they interact and give recommendations. This also serves as your opportunity to improve your product quality and brand image according to the needs and preferences of your customers. In essence, social media allows you to perform a virtual market research conveniently.

How Will Social Media Affect Your Business Reputation?

"It takes a *lifetime* to build
a *reputation* and only
15 minutes to destroy it"

William Buffet

Dave Carroll was flying into Chicago with his band. After they landed, he was informed that baggage handlers were throwing guitar cases around. In one of these cases was his $3500 Taylor guitar, which was damaged in the process. Dave alerted three employees of the airlines what had happened, but was treated with indifference. As if that wasn't enough, Dave spent the next nine months trying to get compensation, but with no success.

But, you know what? Dave decided that he would write a song and create a music video about his experience. He posted the video on YouTube with the title, "United Breaks Guitars". The video received four million views within ten days. Since then he has made two more music videos about the incident.

Since the incident, United Airlines has apologized, but the damage had already been done as soon as Dave made the video. United Airlines reportedly lost 180 million dollars as a result.

Social media blunders can destroy your brand and reputation. This is what happened when Oprah and KFC teamed up to promote KFC's new "Kentucky Grilled Chicken" product with a free coupon. You can probably guess what happened next. Not only did KFC infuriate customers, but they also were one-upped by a competitor. To check out what happened, and see how two other popular companies made blunders, go to www.businessstreamsofincome.com and enter Blunders as the keyword.

With or without your presence, there's no stopping people from talking about your brand through social media websites. Your brand does not belong to you anymore; it only exists in customers' minds, which are massively present in social networks, forums and blogs. When it comes to building your brand reputation, social media can be a double-edged sword. It may benefit or hurt the image of your business at certain times. On one hand, social media enables you to interact directly with your customers. On the other hand, it may prove to be disastrous when overly malicious and negative comments blow out of proportion in social media. In that case, the bad image spreads sooner in social media than in traditional media. Social media results can rank in the top search engine results very quickly. If Joe Schmoe has a bad experience with you and says you suck and it ranks in the top ten search results for your name, then guess what? You Suck. The blame should not be on social media because it merely serves as the means to make your business more visible to your customers.

> The thing about online reputation management is that it is everyone's concern.
>
> An example I saw the other day, searching for the phone number of a local animal hospital, I Googled the business name.
>
> On the first page, I saw a review that said that when a customer took in her cat, she was charged with a bunch of unnecessary expenses.
>
> Online reputation management is EVERY business' problem.

It's critical for businesses to have an ongoing effort to protect what you have worked so hard to build, whether you are a large corporation or a small Mom and Pop Shop. Years of good business can be wiped out by one negative posting that appears on the first page of Google or Yahoo!

You can do something to counteract or prevent negative comments about your business in social media websites. Why not join your customers in their conversations about your brand and products or services? That way, you are able to promote what you have to offer. It also gives you a chance to resolve customer complaints and gives your customers the impression that you are willing to listen to them and that you value their opinions.

In addition, flood the Internet with so much good content that portrays a positive image that will rank highly in the search engines and push negatives lower in the search results.

For New Business Owners That Think You Don't Need to Be Concerned...

The majority of new business owners think that they don't have to be concerned with reputation management because they have a brand new business. They feel that they do not need to worry about their brand right now, because it does not make a difference and nobody knows them (or about their brand) anyway. This kind of thinking could not be more wrong!

The majority of businesses that have a reputation management problem did nothing about it from the start. I don't care what kind of business you have, you will never be able to please 100% of the people all of the time.

There may not be anyone searching for you on the Internet right now, but aren't you planning on it? If you control the first several pages of search results for your brand now, while no one knows about you, it's much easier and cheaper.

Think about this – Let's say your company sells products, and you have 5,000 satisfied customers. You have one customer that didn't get their order on the date you stated on your website. After investigating, you find out it was the shipping company who was at fault, but the customer has already told his friends in the social networks about what happened before you even got a chance to make things right on a problem that you could not control. **Is this fair**? It's not fair if that negative comment ranks in the top 10 of the search results when people type in your brand name when you have had 5,000 other happy customers. Think of how much business a negative comment could cost you. It is your fault though, if it does rank because you didn't do anything about it when you first created your business, and didn't give a second thought to brand/reputation management.

If you can control the search engine page results right now when you are new, this will not even be an issue years down the road because you have established your brand and people only see the stuff you want them to. It will be hard for something negative to get into the top 10 search results with all the content and pages that you have been establishing for the last several years.

That is why it is important to know how to manage your business reputation. Go to www.businessstreamsofincome.com to get a reputation management plan for your business. Just enter the keyword Manage Reputation, or call my office at
1-855-RAINMAKER.

Chapter 2

Online Presence: Creating Buzz About Your Brand

As a business owner, you want people to notice you. The more people who talk about you, the better it is for your business — more so if it earns you a better reputation in the marketplace.

If you want people to talk about you, which is the better way to go: having an online or offline presence? Today, social networking technologies are widely available and over 90% of consumers use the Internet to find information about products and services. Creating an online presence is a must for both online and offline businesses.

Numerous offline businesses do not see the need for creating visibility on the Internet to make people talk about them. They do not appreciate the great earning potential of marketing on the Web or simply fear change. Either way, that mindset won't help a business turn itself from being an unknown to a popular player in the market. Why? Because such businesses will certainly miss the following opportunities that come with using the Internet as a marketing tool:

- **Tapping plenty of niche markets.** Niche marketing, which focuses on a specific segment within a larger customer base, is a more cost-effective and easier way to market your products or services than targeting the mass market.
- **Reaching customers across the globe.** The Internet knows no geographical boundaries, as people from every corner of the world look for goods and services online. For businesses with an online presence, that means more customers and better chances of getting higher income.
- **Interactivity.** Having an online presence opens more doors for communicating directly with most of your customers. That will lead your business to growth and improvement.
- **Using technologies minus the big capital.** Technologies and resources that were once accessible only to large corporations are now within the fingertips of smaller businesses. Such resources, which are made more accessible through the Internet, are used not only for marketing purposes, but also for facilitating business transactions and enhancing customer support.

In this day and age, you have other options besides offline or traditional marketing to promote your business. Thanks to the Internet, you can make your business more visible to your potential customers. Your presence or absence in the World Wide Web can make a huge difference on how your business will take shape in the future, particularly in terms of having more customers and generating more profits. However, the importance of offline marketing should never be discounted. In fact, you may use your online presence to boost your offline marketing efforts. That way, you hit two birds with one stone, as you reach out to both online and offline customers. To learn more about integrating your online and offline marketing, go to www.businessstreamsofincome.com and enter the keyword Create Buzz.

If you don't take advantage of the Internet, your business won't be able to keep up with the competition. You don't want to be left behind, do you?

Chapter 3

Listening to the Buzz: How to Track Your Social Media Presence

Once you have established an online presence, what's next?

It's not enough that you make your brand visible on the Internet and engage your customers through social media sites. You also have to monitor the conversations that take place in social media (e.g. blogs, social networks, etc.) about your brand, products or services, company, and anything that has a direct impact on your business.

After generating buzz about your brand on the Web, now is the time to listen to the buzz going on around your brand. It is extremely important to know what your customers have to say about your brand. Doing so helps you manage and protect your business reputation and understand what people think about your brand and company. Keeping tabs on the social media presence of your business also enables you to respond to customers discussing your brand in social media as well as to discover profit-making opportunities and ways to improve your brand, products or services, and business.

What exactly do people talk about in social media that you have to keep track? The following are the four most common topics of conversations that occur in various social media sites:

1. Compliments

They come in various forms such as positive reviews and

testimonials about your products, services, or customer service. Compliments also include messages of congratulations for any award you received or milestone that your business has achieved. You can use them to build a positive image of your brand and business by posting the testimonials and other compliments on your website or social networking accounts.

2. Criticisms and complaints

More often than not, there are customers who complain about the quality of products or services offered by a certain company. Others are dissatisfied about the incompetent staff or poor customer support. In addition, social media channels are where many customers voice out their disappointment over particular products or brand. Customers usually post negative reviews and comments on blogs, discussion forums, and microblogs.

Instead of fuming over those negative posts, take criticisms and complaints as an opportunity to get your customers' confidence back. Help them find solutions to their problems. Who knows, you might impress your customers with your problem-solving skills and willingness to help them. This will increase positive reviews about your brand and products over time.

On the other hand, if the negative content is slanderous, you can try to get it deleted through legal action if the poster of the content will not remove it, but is very costly, mostly ineffective and can also create negative attention. In most cases, the best course is to produce good content that will rank high in the search engines and will push the negatives lower.

3. The needs of your customers

Your customers may post blog entries, shoutouts, or status messages about what they need, what they are looking for in a certain product, and what things would make them happier. These can serve as your cues when planning which products to sell or how to improve your customer service.

4. Competitors

You should watch not only those things that people say about you or your business, but also any information about your new and existing competitors. It pays to monitor what customers say about products or services from competitors as well as comments that are both favorable and unfavorable to them. That way, you can strategize your future moves in the industry.

5. Infringement of your trademark

If you have a registered trademark, send a cease-and-desist letter to anyone who illegally uses your brand. Informing the infringer that your brand name is trademarked will often prevent having to take legal action. Many startups will bring new products and services to the market without checking to see if the brand name is already taken.

Now that you know what to watch out for, here are the steps you can take to monitor your brand's performance in social media.

- **Determine the keywords for your brand**. The first step to know how your brand fares in social media is to target the right terms or keywords. Your keywords should include the following: your brand name, product name, usual misspellings of the brand and product, relevant or semantically related keywords, brand names of competitors, and usual misspellings of competitor brand. A number of online tools can generate the commonly searched keywords that are related to your brand.
- **Find forums and blogs that mention your brand.** The best places on the Internet to communicate with consumers are forums and blogs. They allow quick exchange of

messages and comments and are frequently read by many Internet users. Aside from keeping track of discussions about your brand in forums and blogs, you can also introduce or promote your products to consumers who might be interested in them. There are different tools available to help you monitor how your brand is perceived in blogs and forums. An example is a comment aggregator that keeps track of the comments made on blogs or forums that mention your brand. Some tools even come up with a thread of conversations that began on one blog and lead to other bloggers replying with posts on their blogs.

- **Check how popular your brand is across the Web.** Free tools such as Google Trends allow you to see the buzz around your brand, as well as the online news articles that mention it.

- **Create email and social media alerts.** Various free tools and services send the most recent results that are relevant to your brand—straight to your inbox. When you set up an email alert, you automatically and regularly receive alerts whenever your brand is mentioned online. Using email alerts such as Google Alerts makes it a lot easier for you to track your brand's online presence without the need to perform regular online searches. Some free alerts like SocialMention are designed specifically for tracking your brand in social media channels such as social bookmarking sites, blogs, and microblogs.

- **Use a social media aggregator.** Get a snapshot of how your brand is being talked about across different social media channels with the help of a social media aggregator. This online tool monitors blog comments, tweets, social networking feeds, product reviews, images, and videos that have to do with your brand and then sends them all to you as an email alert.

Chapter 4

Managing Your Online Reputation: Mistakes to Avoid

As you are browsing blogs, forums, tweets, or videos to monitor your brand's performance in social media, you suddenly come across posts like "[*Name of your brand/company*] sucks big time!" and "Don't buy [*name of your product*]. Worst service ever!" Now, what would you do about these negative comments hurled against your brand?

If you have no idea what to do with all the criticisms regarding your brand, you may learn a lesson from the mistakes businesses commit when they see negative comments about them.

- **Ignoring customer complaints.** Complaints like those mentioned above should never be ignored. Your customers are speaking—and you are supposed to listen to them no matter how hurtful their comments may be. As a business owner, you must expect that there will always be unhappy customers. Just because they are upset with your product or service, doesn't mean they do not deserve your attention. As with your satisfied customers, the unhappy ones can still bring you profits if you know how to win their heart back.
- **Outright dismissing negative comments as a hoax.** Well, there's a good chance that some, if not most, of the trash talk about your business that you find online are just false accusations. These may come from your competitors, your former employee who bears a grudge against you, or someone who simply has nothing to do but spread negative remarks on the Internet. So you dismiss those attacks altogether. But how sure are you that all those are plain hoaxes? Some of them may be valid complaints from real customers. Again, you must pay attention to them.
- **Failure to respond to criticisms quickly.** This mistake happens largely because some companies are not efficient enough when monitoring their brand on the Internet. As a result, they cannot immediately address the concerns of their customers. If you respond slowly to customer complaints, chances are they will quickly switch to the products or services of your competitor. Worse, everybody could have read those comments before you do. To keep these from happening, you can take advantage of online brand tracking tools that search for negative reviews about your brand. These tools can send you the results in real

time. That way, you can immediately address the comments before everybody reads them.

- **Failure to say sorry.** Forgive the cliché, but the customer—online or offline—is always right. So, even if you believe it is the customer's fault, do not forget to apologize for the inconvenience you have caused him or her. Make amends, too. You can offer a discount on the customer's next purchase, a gift certificate, or a free package of your product or service.
- **Attacking the person who posted the negative comment.** Whatever you do, don't retaliate with bad words against a customer—that will definitely backfire on your brand image. It will also provoke the person who posted the comment. Breathe. Relax. Resist your urge to lash out at a person whether his comment is true or not. The best way to deal with a criticism is to reply in an objective and professional manner. Explain your side calmly—by doing so, you turn the situation into your favor. The commenter may agree to disagree with you, apologize, or even delete the negative comment.
- **Failure to bury the evidence.** Negative remarks will stay on the Internet for a long time. More and more people, particularly those searching for information about your product or service, may find and read them. You don't want that to happen because you will lose your potential customers. Usually, it is difficult to get rid of all the negative comments posted on blogs, Twitter, or Facebook. However, with good SEO and social media marketing techniques, it is possible to bury unfavorable comments. For example, if someone posts blog rants against your product, you can counter or bury them by posting more blog content that puts your brand in a positive light. In doing so, you make those comments difficult to find on search engines.

Although you cannot control what people say about you in social media, you can take damage-control measures to cushion the effects of negative comments on your brand image and business reputation. Regardless of the strategies you use, make sure you listen to your customers. Be honest with them without being tactless and be calm when responding to complaints. That way, you build goodwill—not hatred or resentment—with your customers.

One important thing you have to realize about online reputation management: negative comments are not bad at all for your business. In fact, criticisms may have positive effects on your business if you address them properly. They provide you with honest feedback from your customers. How would you know your areas for improvement if your customers did not complain? Treat customer reviews as a measure of how good or bad your product or service is. Also, use them to improve or fix the problems in your business. Learn from the negative comments about your business and use them as an opportunity for business growth.

Did you know that negative feedback might also build trust and reduce doubts about your products or service? No product or service is perfect—some are simply better than the others are. Negative comments about your brand provide balance to the positive ones. Imagine yourself in the situation of your customers: would you trust a product that elicits only praises from people? Maybe not, since you might doubt if all the positive feedback come from actual customers. In contrast, negative comments serves as a confirmation that customers can live with the flaws of your product, service, or company.

Chapter 5

Building Your Brand Image

At this point, you now have a clear idea of how to create buzz about your brand online, monitor the buzz you have generated, and manage negative comments about your business. Your next concern is how to establish your brand image and business reputation with social media tools.

Social Media Checklist

So how do you get started? Considering the number of social media tools around, you may become overwhelmed with the variety of choices and be confused with where to start. Before you worry about which social media tools and strategies to use for building the reputation of your business, you need to figure out first the answers to the following questions:

HigherResultsMarketing.com

1. Is your company ready for social networking?
2. What does your brand stand for?
   (e.g. innovation, safety, convenience, etc.)
3. How much do you know your target audience?
4. How much does your target audience know about you? Have people ever heard about you?
5. How does your target audience use social media websites?
6. How will you reach out to your target audience?
7. Have you determined the risks of using social media tools for your business?
8. Do you have clear goals for implementing social media strategies? What are you trying to achieve?
   (e.g. brand awareness, sales, leads, conversions, etc.)
9. Where are you going to have an online presence? What type of social media can help you accomplish your goals?
10. Who is tasked to maintain your social media presence?
11. How will you engage people and make them notice your presence in social media? Do you have enough resources to do it?
12. How will your social media plan fit into your overall marketing campaign?
13. How will you measure social media success?
    (e.g. comments, subscribers, followers, site/profile views, etc.)

Once you have all the answers to the questions above, you will become more confident when you develop a social media plan for your business. If you are ready to put together your social media plan, go to www.businessstreamsofincome.com and enter the keyword Social Checklist.

Steps to Build a Stronger Reputation for Your Business

How can you make your business popular in social media? The following steps will show you how to make it big in the online world with the help of social media tools:

1. **Establish a strong visibility in various social media channels.**

Make your business visible by creating your social media profiles in multiple social media channels such as blogs, forums, podcasts, and social networking sites. Then integrate all your profiles so that more people will find them and associate them with your website or brand.

2. **Maintain an active participation in social media.**

Social media presence is further strengthened if you participate in social media. The more time you spend in social media, the better for your brand presence. For instance, if you constantly post relevant replies in blogs and forums, more and more people will start to recognize you. Brand recognition or familiarity opens more doors to make your brand known to more people. Of course, you want people to see your profile in social media, but isn't it better if they recognize you as well?

Be sure that you will be able to sustain your social media presence for a long time. It is impractical to become active in a forum for several weeks and then become inactive for a couple of months. If you do so, you will find it hard to reestablish contact with other social media users when you come back.

Thus, you should not be too complacent when people start to recognize your brand in social media. Continue building your social media presence. Spread your visibility across social media channels. It takes a lot of time and effort, but you will certainly be rewarded for it over time.

3. Trade attention with other social media users.

When you build a strong presence for your business, think of it as something that requires you to become a social being in the world of social media. Show other social media users that you are also interested in them. Reciprocate any favor given to you. For instance, if someone promotes your brand or links to your social media profile, return the favor by linking to his or her profile as well.

4. Communicate.

Speak. Listen. Interact. Always be open to communication in social media. Communication is an essential component of relationships with your target customers. Make yourself available to people who want to contact you by sharing your contact details such as telephone numbers, email address, and even your website or blog. In doing so, you spread the presence of your brand to more people. Another benefit you can get from interacting with your fellow social media users is that you learn something new and enhance your social media experience. Isn't it also fun to talk to other people who share the same interest as yours?

5. Provide value to your target customers.

In this step, your goal is to earn trust and credibility as a brand. Providing value to the community can achieve that exactly. Show your fellow social media users that you are not out to take advantage of them.

For example, you do not develop a good reputation by spamming people with your own articles or press releases. Trying to promote your affiliate link or driving traffic to your site may turn potential customers off. Instead, you can submit stories from other websites, but make sure people will find them interesting and relevant to their lives. In addition, you can provide useful and informative content—for sure, people will appreciate you for that. Keep your focus away from benefitting through social media. That way, people will trust and see you as a credible brand.

6. Show your integrity.

Break the rules set by every social media platform and you will damage your business reputation. When you violate the rules, people might notice it. Of course, that will hurt your brand's image on the Web. Behave properly whenever you use social media sites. Avoid spamming and posting irrelevant or plagiarized content. Make sure everything you post or share with others is legitimate. Your business reputation is at stake, so try your best not to damage it in any way.

Establishing your brand involves taking care of your brand image in social media. Remember, everything you do in social media is important. One simple mistake may compromise your business reputation. Therefore, it pays to be careful and active in the social media world.

If you don't know where to start, I will show you how you can build a relationship with your potential customers.

You can go see the video here:
http://www.HigherResultsMarketing.com/freeseminar

Chapter 6

17 Social Media Strategies to Build and Brand Your Business

Now, let's get to the core of social media marketing. You have a variety of options when it comes to social media tools that you can use to position your business as the leader in the industry and to make yourself the person to do business with.

In this chapter, the 17 available social media tools online are discussed in detail, with explanation of how to implement each of them as part of your social media strategy.

Way #1

How to Win Friends and Influence People in the Blogosphere

Among all social media tools, the blog is the most powerful.

Many businesses, however, make the mistake of focusing on social networks such as Twitter and Facebook when they start their social media strategy. They tend to forget how important having a blog is when launching an online campaign.

Here's one big reason to start your social media campaign with blogging: it gives your brand visibility and awareness its much-needed boost.

Your blog can keep your existing and future customers engaged with you and your business. You achieve that purpose by starting a blog that will regularly inform people on everything regarding your business: what's new, what changes they should expect, how you intend to improve your products or services, advertising special offers and so on. By keeping your visitors updated, you show to them that your business is dynamic and moving forward rather than being stagnant.

Posting creative, compelling, and informative content on your blog provides value to consumers. You can also post your opinions and insights about the most pressing issues about your industry and anything that concerns your target audience. That way, you make yourself an authority on a certain field. When people start to appreciate and trust you, it's a sign that your business is gradually earning a better online reputation. And like social networking sites, a blog gives you the chance to connect with consumers on a personal level and help you turn visitors into loyal customers. Include a lead capture or opt-in and offer something very valuable for FREE that will entice them to sign up to your list. This will enable you to start building your list of interested prospects. Not only do you want to brand yourself, but also you want to get everyone who is interested in what you have to say, into your sales funnel.

Unfortunately, there's a downside to blogging—though it is not entirely the blog's fault. Blogging is a great social media strategy only if you supply your blog with fresh, relevant, and updated content regularly. Otherwise, your blog will become a relic of the Internet's past. If you think you will run out of things to say in the long run and cannot sustain the enthusiasm and interest of your blog visitors, then there is no point in creating a blog in the first place. An ideal solution to that, especially if you are not confident enough of your writing skill, is to hire a writer to create content for your blog.

Thus, it is very important to give blogging a careful thought before you set up your own blog. Create clearcut goals and plans for using your blog to jumpstart your social media campaign. Of course, your blog content should be related to your business.

During the planning process, ask yourself these questions:

- Do you think your blog will be picked up by the online audience?
- What do your existing and potential customers want from your blog?
- What will be your blog's name? (While naming your blog seems like a trivial decision, it is crucial for your branding.)
- What tone will you set for your blog content? (e.g. formal vs. informal, authoritative vs. conversational, detached vs. personal, etc.)
- What will your blog look like?
- How often will you post in your blog?
- How will you keep your visitors coming back?

Setting Up Your Own Blog

Creating a blog is easy even for those who have only basic knowledge about computers and the Internet. Blogging is an ideal way for businesses to promote their brand.

Your blog's name will serve as the overall theme of the blog. It is important in helping search engines drive traffic to your blog so that more people will visit it. That being said, you must invest time and energy in coming up with a great name for your blog. When you choose a name for your blog, make sure it reflects your brand image as well as the products or services that you are promoting.

In addition, include a good keyword or key phrase in it. Here's an example: if you are selling natural weight loss products, your blog name could be something similar to "Natural Weight Loss (or Fat Burning/Lose Weight) Secrets Revealed."

Another important element is the blog description. As the term suggests, a blog description describes in a line or two what your blog is all about. Search engines use that description when they pick up your blog and include it in the search results when people do keyword search online. Going back to the example given above, the fitting description would be somewhere along the lines of "Useful information and tips on losing weight the natural way."

Now, for the content of your blog. You need to provide plenty of useful information. You can post a variety of topics so that your blog won't sound monotonous and look boring. For the natural weight loss blog, you can include tips on dieting, exercising, taking herbal supplements, and other ways to lose weight. To add variety to your blog, you can add reviews on several weight loss programs that you are marketing as well as trivia and other interesting facts about losing weight and staying fit.

Make sure that in your blog, you place links that take your visitors directly to your main product website. If your readers are interested in knowing more about your product, all they have to do is click the link to your product website. You will waste the opportunity to introduce your products to your target customers if you do not add links in your blog posts.

Responding to Comments on Your Blog

Thou shall reply to comments that are posted on your blog. This is one cardinal rule you have to observe when blogging to promote your business. What's the use of your numerous page views and blog comments if you do not pay attention to them?

But why bother to respond, you might ask. Think of it as something that can enhance your brand image on the Web. Responding to blog comments is your way of letting your visitors know that you actually exist—not as a spammer but as a legitimate blogger—and are interested in what they have to say. When a visitor leaves a comment on your blog, never think twice about replying to it. When you do so, you give that visitor a good reason to visit your blog again.

If you were in the shoes of your blog visitors, wouldn't you be discouraged to visit the blog again if its owner seemed not to care about your comment? Ignoring comments is plain rude and unprofessional, so take time to respond to comments on your blog even if your schedule is hectic. Better yet, click on the link of your commenter to see his or her blog and leave a comment there. For sure, the commenter will come back to your blog and continue your conversation.

But what about offensive comments? If you reply with an equally or more aggressive attack, you will only invite more harsh comments from the hostile commenter. That's simply a waste of time and energy. What you can do is to step back, breathe, and get back when you are no longer emotional about it. If a commenter points out a mistake in your blog or makes a valid accusation, correct your mistake, apologize, and thank him or her for the heads-up. Do not take attacks personally lest they will make the flame bigger. Accept the reality that some people will disagree with you. The best way to deal with negative remarks is to respond in a collected, reasonable, and professional fashion. Choose your words carefully to make them sound neutral instead of combative.

Posting Comments to Other Influential Blogs

Aside from replying to comments posted on your blog, it is also good to be on the other side of the equation: posting a comment to other blogs. But don't just post comments on any blog—be sure that you do it only on influential blogs.

What is an influential blog, anyway? It is a blog that not only has a huge following on the Internet, but is also widely known and respected in the industry where it belongs. It has the ability to inspire and motivate a lot of people. Almost everything that an influential blogger says becomes news and are believed by most people. Anything it recommends or promotes will enjoy a good reception from the public.

This is where posting comments to influential blogs becomes necessary. Leave a comment on another blog, and you will be noticed. It is the first step to gaining endorsements from the powerful players in the industry. If an influential blogger takes notice of you and is impressed with the quality of your brand, chances are he or she will feature or promote you. That will benefit your brand's image a lot. On top of that, since influential blogs are read by many people, you also gain more exposure on the Internet.

A few reminders, though. First, forget about aggressively promoting your brand in your comment to other blogs. When you write your comment, avoid making it sound like spam. Second, if you have to post a negative comment (which is perfectly all right), be careful with your tone and word choice. You don't want to appear hostile to someone who might help you promote your business, right? Finally and most importantly, do not forget to include your name and a link to your blog when you post your comment. You are less likely to get feedback if you post a comment anonymously. Also, the link is important because it helps deliver more traffic to your blog.

Way #2

Discover the Fortune That Lies Hidden in Email

Email is a useful tool for social networking. That is why some businesses take advantage of it to make their brand known by more Internet users. They use email as their bridge to reach out to potential customers directly and quickly. Email has been recognized as an effective means to communicate with existing and prospective customers on a personal level and to make them aware of the existence of your brand.

Email turns your prospects into buyers by using a lead capture system. It puts your prospects into a sales funnel that helps you stay connected with your prospects and customers. It's like a virtual employee that is working 24/7 for your business.

Email marketing is particularly associated with distribution of newsletters to the subscribers of a business. Typically, newsletters contain news about a company's latest products, improvements to existing ones, interesting information or special deals. People, who are interested, sign up for a newsletter, and they receive them in their inbox on a regular basis. Replying to emails is convenient as well for consumers. All such benefits make email marketing a reliable and cost-effective way to market a brand, product, or service.

Integrating Email to Your Social Media Marketing Mix

Never underestimate the power of email in promoting your business. In fact, you can integrate email into your social media marketing plan to make it more effective. Using email as part of a social media marketing campaign is a growing trend in the online world nowadays. In essence, it involves sharing information or content over email to trigger a series of replies or conversations.

Are you interested in implementing your email campaign with your social media marketing strategy? Keep the following tips in mind:

- **Figure out the things that encourage people to share information.** The following are the common reasons that motivate people to share content with their contacts: rewards, a sense of belongingness within an online community, a sense of confidence, and a feel-good effect. Once you have understood them, you will know what to do to trigger a continuous exchange of information over email.

- **Teach your email subscribers how to share content.** Believe it or not, sharing through email is still a foreign concept among many Internet users. Encourage people to share your content by educating them on how to do so. Adding links to your email is not enough. You may consider including a "What's this?" button along with the "Share this" button to your email. Make sure that you give clear and detailed instructions on how to use the sharing feature.

- **Focus on the right social networks.** Choose only the social media websites where your target customers spend most of their time interacting and sharing content with others. Do your research by tracking network activity, making market surveys, and testing share activity. Also, you need to determine the right number of social networks to target. All these steps ensure that you won't waste your time, effort, and resources on social networks that your target audience does not use.

- **Create valuable and "share worthy" content.** People are not likely to share something they think is crap. Put meat to your content so that people will pick it up and share to their networks over email and social media. Make sure the content is easy to grasp and interesting to your target audience. You may even want to offer incentives or rewards every time a person shares your content with other people.

- **Take advantage of the social marketing features of your email software provider.** They make it easier for you to send emails directly to your social network accounts like Facebook.

- **Promote your email newsletter through your social networks.** You can publicize your newsletter by posting a status update on your social networks such as Facebook, Twitter, or LinkedIn before you make an email send out. In doing so, you get your target audience excited or curious about the release of your newsletter.

- **Monitor your business or brand in social networks.** That way, you get an idea of how to strengthen your email marketing campaign. Social networks such as Twitter,

LinkedIn, and Facebook have search options that allow you to track everything that mentions your business. For example, if you find a complaint about your products, you may create an email send out that states how you are going to address the complaint.

- **Establish yourself as an authority.** Join groups in various social media sites and get yourself involved in discussions. Give your expert opinion and advice about topics that your target audience deem important. If you are successful in making yourself a trusted source of information, people will become more interested or even excited in what you have to say.

To learn more about how to use the power of email marketing, I have a free report that will show you how. Just go to www.businessstreamsofincome.com and enter Email Marketing as the keyword.

Way #3

Become a Video Marketing Star

What is the first thing that usually comes to mind when talking about video sharing sites? You guessed it right—YouTube. This site has an impact on the way people use the Internet. However, there are tons of other popular video sharing sites that enable people to upload and view videos online.

For your business, using video sharing sites is a great way to promote your brand, products, or services.

Now check this out:

FORD Modeling Agency

Increased their sales in one year by over 140% just by using "reality-style" videos on YouTube.

Aside from video sharing sites, you may also upload your promotional videos on your website. An effective video marketing strategy involves the use of brief, interesting, and informative videos to increase brand awareness and online presence of a business. This is possible because videos are included in search engine results.

Besides brand awareness, video marketing offers a variety of other benefits. First, it has a high educational value, just like written content. Through videos, you can show consumers how beneficial your product or service is and how to use it properly. Because most people prefer watching videos than reading articles, videos fare better in engaging more consumers than online content. Lastly, video marketing is easier than it seems. Good thing there are various technologies such as editing, post-production, and video posting services that make the job easy for you.

Listed here are five tips to help make your video marketing campaign work:

1. Keep the video short and catchy.

    It should be shorter than the usual 30-second commercial spot on TV. Internet users are less patient than TV viewers are, so to speak. Ideally, keep your video around 5 to 15 minutes long.

2. Make sure that your message is consistent and appropriate for the medium.

    Avoid merely duplicating your advertisements across different media such as TV and banner ads.

3. Offer your videos in various formats.

    Since Internet users have different types of video players, it pays to offer your video in multiple formats so that more people can play them.

4. Make sure that your brand is prominently shown or watermarked in the entire video.

That way, you boost your brand recognition among consumers.

5. Measure your video marketing success.

In doing so, you can determine if your video marketing efforts are effective, what needs to be improved, and if the campaign is worth pursuing. Measure your video marketing campaign performance in terms of number of views, interaction rates, and conversion rates.

See how you can make more impact and gain more profit in your business using video marketing.

Here is another example:

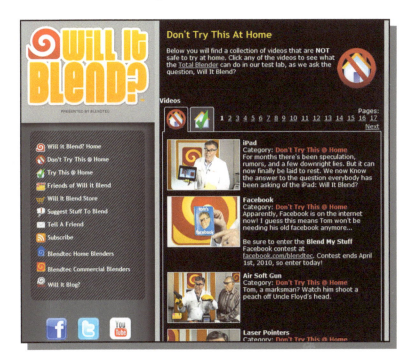

Blendtec knew that they had the best blender in the world, but people didn't know who they were. So, they set out to create brand awareness by filming 5 videos.

Was it successful?

5 days after posting the videos on their WillItBlend website and on YouTube, they reached 6 million views.

As their videos on YouTube grew in popularity, Blendtec found their online sales grew by 500%.

To find out what they did that got this much attention, go to www.businessstreamsofincome.com. Just enter the keyword Video Marketing.

How could you use video marketing in your business?

Way #4

Social Networks Are the New Media

In the United States, millions of Internet users visit popular social networking websites such as Facebook and Twitter on any given day. These social networks are specialized sites that suit the specific interests of its users, unlike YouTube and MySpace that have a mass appeal. The sheer number of social networking users and the highly targeted audiences coming from specialized sites offer opportunities to businesses that cater to a segment of a mass market.

As part of your social media campaign, social networking sites can boost your brand image and your product sales. The key to ensure success is choosing the right social networks to find your target audience. You must also plan strategies that convert followers and fans to leads and customers. Customized pages on your social networking accounts can also directly increase your ability to collect and message leads and boost sales.

Three of these social networking sites are Twitter, Facebook, and LinkedIn.

Twitter

Everybody is raving about Twitter, so much so that it was declared the most popular English word in 2009. I'm not kidding. So what does it mean to you as a business owner? A lot! Twitter is a microblog that has the same marketing potential as a blog, though its content is much shorter and snappier. With Twitter, you can easily connect to your existing and future customers in real-time not only through the Internet, but also through mobile phones and desktop applications. What's more, Twitter enables you to address the needs of your target audience right away. In this day and age when almost everything is done in just a few clicks, a swift response is all you need to gain credibility and to outdo the competition.

Here are some tips to maximize your marketing efforts with Twitter:

1. Determine the kind of information you will post on Twitter and how you will respond to the messages from people.

2. Tweet often but don't spam. This means you need to post relevant and informative content that your target audience may use. Spamming will just turn off potential customers.

3. Avoid posting a lot of overt sales pitches. Your target customers won't appreciate that.

4. Maximize your profile page so that your followers will get to know about your brand and business.

5. An important part of marketing your brand via Twitter is conversation. Ask good questions, initiate conversations, and take polls.

6. Follow the Twitter feeds of your potential customers. This is a great way to make them notice you and your business.

A good example of a company that is benefiting from the use of Twitter is Dell Outlet.

Dell Outlet carries refurbished equipment and other inventory that it needs to sell quickly. They often post offers on Twitter that are exclusive to their Twitter followers. They twitter only a few times a week so they don't spam their followers, and they use tracking URLs to gauge what followers like most.

Do the coupons work? Big time.

Dell Outlet has made more than $3 million in revenue that they attribute to their Twitter posts.

Another great example:

Naked Pizza, a New Orleans restaurant, has done a successful campaign to create over 4300 followers who are in the surrounding area.

They replaced their "call for delivery" billboard above their restaurant with a large Twitter bird inviting passersby to follow Naked Pizza for special deals.

Naked Pizza has attributed $2 million, which is 20% of their annual revenue to Twitter.

Facebook

Another great social network to tap for your social media campaign is Facebook. With hundreds of millions of users, it's worth it to invest your time and energy with marketing through Facebook mainly because it delivers the most loyal visitors. And get this: A study has shown that Facebook tops other social networking sites in terms of visitor loyalty.

Would you like some of this action?

Now pay attention to this:

An effective marketing strategy is to create a Facebook Page of your product, service, or company. A Facebook Page enables you to establish your own community online, which works just like Twitter. But compared to Twitter, Facebook gives more options for customization.

Facebook's strength lies in its capability as a viral marketing tool. When your fans get in touch with you on Facebook, their friends will be able to view the comments on their news feed. How's that for more publicity for your business?

To keep your target audience engaged, you have to update your Facebook Page status as often as you can. Provide updates on your brand or company, helpful tips on things related to your industry, and any announcement you wish to make. Give them a reason to check your Facebook Page frequently and be interested in what you are going to say. Also, encourage them to let you know about their feedback on whatever you are selling.

Holding contests and offering coupons are two of the best ways to entice other Facebook users to like and follow your page.

Check out Papa John's Facebook Page at
www.facebook.com/papajohns

Sales improved by more than 28%. Incentives like "free pizzas for friends" helped them double their fan base in a single month.

LinkedIn

Like Facebook and Twitter, LinkedIn is a popular niche social network. LinkedIn is a reliable and useful tool to reach out to a segment of the mass market with certain interests. With this social media tool, you can do these three strategies for marketing your brand: improve the presence and awareness of your brand and business, get more traffic and assistance on your SEO (search engine optimization) campaign, and generate sales leads.

Using LinkedIn as part of your social media marketing mix is a wise move because of the unique benefits it can provide to your business. For one, LinkedIn allows you to perform market research through its Q&A feature. This comes in handy when you need to know how much the demand is for the type of product you are going to introduce in the market. When it comes to keeping track of your competitors, LinkedIn does the job for you efficiently. It enables you to view the staff, clients, recent moves, and other competitor information that are otherwise not readily available to you. That means you can design your marketing campaign, taking into account what the competition does.

Social networks can be very powerful, but just like any marketing strategy, social media needs planning.

To get your Free Profit Explosion consultation, go to www.HigherResultsMarketing.com/freestrategysession, or call my office at 1-855-RAINMAKER.

Way #5

Content Is King

It doesn't take a marketing genius to know how important content is in promoting a business on the Internet. True enough, content reigns supreme in the online marketing kingdom, and the same holds true in social media marketing. Without compelling and engaging content, your blog will just be a nobody on the Web, your tweets will go unnoticed, and your press releases won't get the sales leads you want. Content carries information relevant to your potential customers. You use it to grab their attention and hopefully, to generate sales from them.

Are you eager to know how to ensure your success as a social media marketer? Give what social media users crave: high-quality content. The following are surefire ways to make your content a hit, regardless of what you are writing (e.g. white papers, ebooks, blog posts, Facebook status updates, tweets, etc.).

- **Research.** You cannot just start writing without research. For social media, this entails knowing who your audience is and the kind of content that social media users would like to read.

- **Create a compelling headline.** Plenty of content is generated in social media channels every single day. How will you stand out from the rest? Simple: write a headline that will hook more social media users into reading your content.

- **Create a startling opening statement.** This will rouse your readers' curiosity and will make them want to read more.

- **Keep a friendly, conversational tone.** Remember, the important word in social media marketing is "social." So talk to your audience as you would to a friend. Instead of a detached, stiff tone, opt for more personal and interactive content.

- **Avoid talking like an aggressive salesperson.** Overly promoting your business in your content will do more harm than good, as social media users typically ignore overt sales pitches. If you want people to pay attention to you, try to give substantial and helpful information they can actually use.

- **Do away with fluff.** Social media users are not forgiving when it comes to fluff. They want to get the gist of your content within only a few minutes or even in just one glance if it is for microblogs. Keep your readers' short attention span in mind. Spare them the agony of reading a bulk of meaningless text by removing all the unnecessary words or sentences from your content.

- **Make yourself an expert resource in your field.** How? Offer an in-depth analysis or opinion that is not available elsewhere. By being the trusted resource, you earn credibility for the brand you represent.

- **Learn from your mistakes.** If you fail for the first time, do not be discouraged. Consider that as your opportunity to learn so that next time, you know exactly how to capture the attention of your target audience.

Way #6

Want to Be on Page 1 of Google?

Any social media marketing plan is not complete without SEO (Search Engine Optimization). Social media and SEO make for a perfect combination in boosting your brand's presence on the Internet. You need both to steer your business to long-term success.

The right SEO techniques can help your brand land on the first page of search engine results, giving you a competitive edge in the market and getting more traffic. Getting more traffic to your website means more sales for your business.

There is a great report at www.businessstreamsofincome.com called "10 Sure-Fire Tips to Get on the First Page of Google". To get it, just enter the keyword Google Page 1.

The biggest percentage of search engine users will most likely find what they are looking for on the first page of the search results. What people find on the first page of Google will have an affect on whether they feel that you have a positive or negative reputation. This can determine whether someone buys your products or services.

Social media content tends to rank very well in the search engines. So how does SEO help enhance your social media marketing campaign? The heart of any SEO strategy is keyword research— you have to know what your potential customers are looking for over the Internet. Once you have done so, it will be easy for you to design your social media campaign based on your keyword research.

An SEO technique used by many social media marketers is including keywords in all the content they submit to social media sites. Use keywords in your blog posts, tweets, Facebook status updates, LinkedIn profile, as well as titles and descriptions of videos and photos you upload in video and photo sharing sites. Using keywords properly can help consumers find you in social media sites.

SEO also facilitates the viral marketing component of a social media campaign. People who like your blog post or your video might share the link through their social networks. In viral marketing combined with SEO strategies, social media users themselves promote your brand to others. Isn't that a great idea?

Another important SEO component that you should not miss on your social media campaign is active participation in online communities. You do that by commenting on blogs and other social networks and placing your links to raise your chance of being noticed by your target customers.

The key to get more online exposure for your brand is choosing the appropriate SEO strategies to implement with your social media marketing campaign. Everything you do in social media sites should be optimized for search engines so that your brand can enjoy a high ranking in search engines.

Social media depends a lot on SEO, just like how SEO depends on social media. As a smart business owner, you have to be knowledgeable on both fields to ensure maximum online visibility for your business.

Way #7

Your Customers Are Looking Locally for You

It's great to be able to find your potential customers online, right? But wouldn't it be better if your prospects find you instead? Thanks to local map listings, you can achieve just that.

Nowadays, an increasing number of Internet users are looking for local businesses over the Web. Most of them prefer local results than organic and paid listings on search engine results. To enhance the online presence of your business, you must seriously consider using local map listings as part of your social media marketing strategy.

Local map listings such as Google Places are the Yellow Pages of the online world. Consumers who are looking for a certain type of business can find what they need by using search engines, which generate local map listings related to the searched term. An Internet user can easily see a local map listing—it appears on the top right side of the search result page above the paid listings. For example, if a person wants to look for an orthodontist in Portland, Or, he or she will have to use the Google search engine, which will come up with a map and links of the different orthodontists in Portland, Or.

Are you interested in making your business land on the first page of Google search results? You may consider signing up for Google Places. This will assure you that your site will appear at the top of Google search results beside a map when people search for a business similar to yours.

Get our special report on Google Places at www.businessstreamsofincome.com. Enter the keyword Google Places.

Once your business is included in the local business directory of Google, people who have a Google account may do reviews about your company and give you a rating. The higher rating you get, the easier it will be for people to find your business in local map listings.

To maximize your exposure online, focus your goal on getting a higher rank in Google map listings. You need to do three things to meet this goal. First, you have to encourage more people to write reviews about your business. Second, you must make sure that your location keywords (e.g. hotels in Louisville, Kentucky, car rental services in Sarasota, Florida, etc.) are added in the local business listing. Third, include more photos and videos to your account with Google Places.

Way #8

Who Else Wants to Reach the Press?

In the past when traditional marketing was the sole option for companies, press releases used to be exclusive to journalists. Today, with the advent of social media, press releases have become accessible to consumers as well. Bloggers, online forum members, and even ordinary Internet users can get first-hand information about what a company has been up to. Thanks to social media channels, these people not only enjoy access to press releases, but also have the power to distribute press releases to their social media community.

More aptly called social media releases, press releases are an indispensable addition to the social media marketing mix of any type of business. Companies distribute press releases to a broad range of news websites to inform not only their target customers but also the whole world about what they have to offer. For their part, blogs, forums, microblogs, and other social networks pick them up and spread the word. Press releases also have a tendency to rank well in Google search results. Aside from ease of access and distribution, social media releases do not cost much time and money to do.

If you are just starting out your business, your first social media releases must contain news about the launch of your business, including information about the products or services you are selling. For the subsequent social media releases, you can give updates about changes in your business, improvements or upgrades in your products or services, and any promo or discounts you offer to your customers.

However, here's a big challenge that awaits you as you are writing a press release: social media users are hard to please. More often than not, they just ignore press releases, especially those brimming with blatant sales pitch, focusing on the company instead of the news itself, and written blandly.

How do you get people interested in what your business has been up to? Write your press releases in such a way that it provides value to your readers. The following are the ways to achieve that:

- **Provide meaningful information.** So, your company has recently launched a new product in the market. So what? Unless you are able to answer this question, your target audience won't easily see the point of reading your press release. Instead of focusing only on the news, clearly explain to your readers the implications and benefits of your newest product line. What will they get from it? How will it improve their lives? Highlight them in your press release.

- **Make it concise and succinct.** State the essential information in the fewest words possible. Remember, you are writing press releases for social media sites, not an epic for a full-length book.

- **Ditch the direct sales pitch.** You are not likely to earn trust from your target audience if you keep on bombarding them with direct sales pitch in your press releases. Do not tell people what they should buy—they are intelligent enough to decide that for themselves.

- **Include your supporting assets.** This will enhance the value of your press releases. Photos of your products and company logo, viral videos, and other marketing materials can improve your visibility on the Internet.

Way #9

Bookmark It!

Over the years, the Internet has undergone many innovations to enhance the Web surfing experience of millions of users. Take social bookmarking for example. Nowadays, people can easily save and rate websites, content, videos, and blogs that they find useful or interesting. Instead of saving bookmarks of their favorite sites on their browser, Internet users may opt to use social bookmarking sites so that they can access their bookmarked sites from any computer anytime.

What does it have to do with my business, you might ask. Well, you can benefit from social bookmarking or tagging in several ways. If you sign up for popular social bookmarking sites, your business will get more online visibility. Social bookmarking is also an ideal way to strengthen your ties with your existing and future customers and to get easy access to new resources for your business.

To get started, you need to subscribe first to at least one social bookmarking site. Some of the most well known tagging sites today include StumbleUpon, Digg, Delicious, and Reddit. Choose a site carefully to make sure that it works with your niche. For that purpose, you must have a clear idea of who your target audience is. Popular social bookmarking sites are recommended since they can deliver the most traffic to your website, thus enhancing your presence on the Internet.

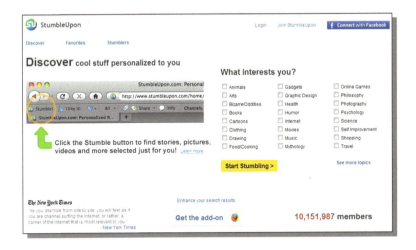

Once you have registered an account in a social bookmarking site, familiarize yourself with features of the site. You can do many things in a social bookmarking site. You may submit content from your blog or website and share bookmarks with your target customers. It is possible to build your own network too. You just have to invite people to add your website to their bookmarks and include you in their network. Social bookmarking sites also allow you to search bookmarks that are useful for the growth of your business.

If used properly, social bookmarking can be a cost-effective marketing tool. There are several things you have to keep in mind when using social bookmarking sites to promote your business:

- **Avoid creating multiple accounts on one social bookmarking site.** Some unscrupulous people open various accounts just so they can vote for themselves many times. Doing so will only hurt the reputation of your business.

- **Submit quality content.** That way, you can get more votes quickly and get high ranking in your social bookmarking site.

- **Avoid spamming.** Spamming won't help your business in any way. Instead, you can ask for help from your friends to promote your business on social bookmarking sites.

Way #10

Use Images/Photos to Show Who You Are

A picture is worth a thousand words, as the saying goes. When it comes to social media marketing, a photo is worth a thousand customers—or even more.

Photo sharing has been a craze on the Internet nowadays. People from all corners of the world share tons of photos over the Web each day for various purposes. Some do it just for fun; others do it to update their family and friends about what they have been up to.

If you are one of those who enjoy uploading and viewing images in photo sharing sites, you might as well take advantage of these sites for your business. On the other hand, if you have never tried it yet, now is the time to use photo sharing sites to enhance the online presence of your business.

Photo sharing refers to transferring or publishing of digital images on the Internet so that they can be shared with others. It offers so many benefits to any business, the most important of which is enabling you to connect and communicate with your existing and potential customers. In addition, it increases online visibility of your business, as it allows you to develop links to your website or blog and to make content and visuals that you can incorporate into your website. You can even tag your photos with addresses to be able to create maps for your website or blog.

That being said, photo sharing makes a lot of sense if you want your business to grow faster. A number of photo sharing sites including Flickr, Photobucket, Google Picassa, and Snapfish can help you establish a strong presence on the Web. The right photo sharing site to use depends on your needs and the features offered such as the amount of photo storage, number of albums, file format supported, integration with social media platforms, customization and uploading options, and ease of storing and editing of images.

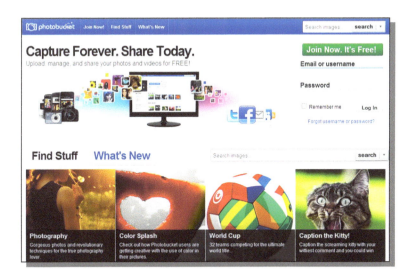

Signing up for photo sharing sites takes only a few minutes, and you can start with a free account that enables you to upload multiple photos right away as long as you do not exceed the limit.

To maximize the marketing potential of photo sharing, here are a few tips to guide you:

- **Select carefully the photos you will post.** Each of your photos is a representation of your brand. The quality of the photos you post speaks volumes about the quality of your business.

- **Create unique Meta titles, Meta descriptions, and Meta tags for every image.** This is an SEO technique that will lead to high search engine rankings for your website, thus making your business more visible on the Web.

- **Take time to create a good profile.** Some photo sharing sites such as Flickr allow subscribers to create a profile that describes their business. On your profile, you can add keyword-rich links that will direct people to your website, blog, or social network profiles.

- **Participate in the community where your target customers can be found.** How will you make people notice you on photo sharing sites? Simple: leave comments on the photos of other users of the site.

- **Build your own network of contacts.** Did you know that you could use photo sharing sites much in the same way as LinkedIn and Facebook? Photo sharing sites allow you to establish your own network made up of people that share the same interests. That way, you can cater more to your niche audience.

- **Post videos.** Some photo sharing sites double as video sharing sites, thus helping you maximize your brand awareness campaign.

Way #11

The Lowdown on Podcasts

A smart business owner knows that the best way to reach out to as many consumers as possible is to leverage new tools or technologies used by many people. Podcasts are among the online technologies that can be tapped to boost the popularity of your business online, improve your market reach, and establish customer loyalty. Podcasts are audio or video media files that can be played on portable media players or on a computer. About 40 million listeners on the Web can access just a single podcast. Imagine that number of customers being driven to your business.

Compared to other social media tools, podcasting technology is still in its infancy. However, it has already been recognized as an effective marketing and communication tool. Podcasting for business involves creating audio content that cover a wide range of topics relevant to many consumers. Listeners who are interested in the information provided by a certain podcast may sign up for a podcasting service.

How does podcasting enhance your social media campaign? It helps you target multi-tasking people who find reading emails and website or blog content too time-consuming. With a podcast, an Internet user can just stream the audio and play it. This allows them to listen to the audio while doing other things on their computer.

The following are important tips to remember before you start using podcasting as a marketing tool:

- **Educate yourself about podcasting.** This technology is a great tool for your business, only if you use it properly.

- **Understand the needs of your target customers.** That way, you can cater to their needs better through podcasting.

- **Have something worthwhile to say.** To stress the point again, your listeners are multi-taskers who do not want their time wasted on a babbling piece of audio. Aside from your listeners' time, you are wasting yours as well, not to mention your energy in creating that podcast. Content in podcasting is no different from website or blog content— you have to make sure that your podcast offers value-added messaging, meaning it should be relevant and useful enough for your target audience.

- **Create podcasts that contain interviews with experts on your niche. Better yet, have someone interview you.** This will quickly position your company as a trusted leader in your industry.

- **Edit your podcasts for length and quality.** Of course, you do not want to bore your listeners to death. Be sure that you use high-quality recording equipment too.

- **Submit your podcasts to search engines and Web directories.** That way, you broaden your customer reach on the Internet.

You can use Blog Talk Radio to record your podcast. That is a free site where anyone can set up a podcast or even have your own radio talk show over the web. Your podcast or radio show will even become available on iTunes.

So what information can you deliver to your target audience in a podcast format? How can you market your podcast to build your brand, produce more leads and differentiate yourself from your competitors?

Go to www.businessstreamsofincome.com and enter the keyword Podcast or call my office at 1-855-RAINMAKER to see the ways that you can use podcasts to benefit your business.

Way #12

Put Your Presentation Online

Business presentations have long been a staple in boardrooms and conference halls. Then came social media and changed the way presentations are being used. Today, business executives are not the only ones that can view business presentations. Even consumers can do that in the comfort of their own home by visiting presentation sharing sites.

Slowly but surely, online presentations have been used by more and more businesses as part of their marketing and communication strategy. These online presentations are uploaded, shared, and viewed on presentation sharing sites, which are visited by Internet users who are searching for information they need. Presentation sharing sites are similar to photo sharing and video sharing sites in the sense that they serve as venues for sharing content to millions of Internet users. The goals of businesses that use these sites are almost the same too. All of these sites are tapped to raise brand awareness, ensure customer loyalty, and sometimes to generate sales. The only difference is the content being shared in these sites. In the case of presentation sharing sites, the content comes in the form of slide presentations.

Some of the most popular presentation sharing sites today include SlideShare, Scribd, Google Presentations, and Docstoc. Except for Google Presentations, all of these presentation sites support not only slide presentations, but also documents in Word and PDF formats, templates, ebooks, manuals, and forms. Some presentation sharing sites offer value-added services to their clients. For example, SlideShare allows its users to create webinars (Web-based seminars) and add audio files to them. As a new social media marketer, you will realize how important webinars are in generating leads and sales for your company.

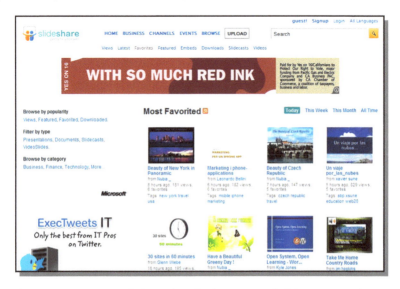

Various reasons explain why it is a good idea to make your business known to your target audience through presentation sharing sites. For one, sharing presentations online gives you the chance to connect to millions of Internet users. As with blogging and social networking, presentation sharing sites also enable you to post comments on other presentations as well as receive comments from others. Aside from connecting and interacting with potential customers, you can also participate in communities with which you share the same business goals. The presentations that you upload in these sites can be embedded into your website, blog, and social network accounts. The best thing about using presentation sharing sites for your marketing campaign is that it does not cost you much.

So how do you start? The following are the basic steps in using presentation sharing sites for your marketing campaign.

1. Open an account using the name of your company.
2. Create a profile complete with information about your business. Add a photo, address, and link to your website.
3. Upload well-executed presentations, market reports, survey results, and everything that your target customers may want to view. Before uploading, check if you have included the title, description, and tags for every presentation or document.
4. Let consumers know that you are using a presentation sharing site to post all of your public presentations. You can share the news through press releases, your social media networks, blog, and website.

Way #13

Profits That Lie Hidden in Forums

Online forums should be on top of your social media marketing priorities if you want to target a specific niche market. If you are a frequent Internet user, this fact should be a no-brainer for you. Over the Internet, you can find various discussion forums, each catering to a specific interest. For example, there are forums made for women, vintage car owners, basketball fans, online gaming enthusiasts, and a lot more.

Also known as message boards, online forums can be a fun yet worthwhile way to market your business effectively to a highly targeted audience. Forums give you an opportunity to promote anything you have to offer without the use of aggressive advertising tactics. You can build your credibility by answering questions in forums that are related to your industry. Doing so gives other forum members the impression that you are an expert and therefore worthy of their trust.

Participating in forums does not only benefit you in terms of marketing your brand. It also offers valuable insights on what your target customers need, what they are looking for in a product or service, and what they think about your company. Forums keep you abreast of the latest trends in your industry, which can help your business keep up with the times.

To begin with forum marketing, you need to find a forum that interests you and where your target audience frequents. A simple online search will take you to the right forums where you can promote your business. Once you have found the right forum, it would be better to just lurk around first rather than to post messages right away. That way, you can figure out the tone of the forum and make sure that it is really the right place to market your brand.

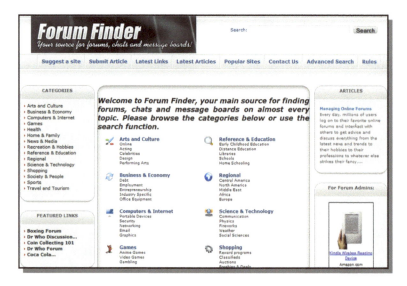

At this point, you still cannot post your opinions or answers to questions on the forum. Of course, you have to introduce yourself first and give some background details about yourself. In doing so, forum members won't mistake you for a spammer. Once you are welcomed, you can start posting messages on the forum.

In any online forum, certain rules have to be observed. You must follow the etiquettes of posting in forums because you carry the reputation of your business. Once you mess it up, you will find it hard to gain the trust of other forum members again. Here are a few tips to keep in mind:

- **Include your name, contact details, and website or blog URL in your signature line.** This is a more acceptable way to promote your business than attaching banner ads to your signature line. Attaching a signature line to all your forum posts helps in making people recognize your brand.

- **Offer help when possible.** This will make people notice and like you.

- **No personal attacks, please.** Although forums are designed to be a venue for open discussions, there are certain limits to it. Harsh attacks are an example. If people start taking potshots at your company or product, fight the urge to reply aggressively. Of course, you can always defend your side, but make sure you do so in a calm, professional manner.

- **Avoid posting blatant advertisements.** People do not want to be told what to buy—they want to know the ways to improve their lives.

Way #14

The Secret of Making People Like You: Your Own Membership Site

Do you want to know an effective way to build your social networks? Setting up your own membership site not only widens your reach in social media, but also gives you the chance to earn extra income.

In essence, a membership site is a website where people access exclusive content from a password-protected section in exchange for a certain amount. Contrary to what you might think, people are willing to spend money for online content. The content you will offer to your subscribers may come in the form of information, articles, videos, audios, music, software, ebooks, and even games.

Does this seem to be an attractive option for your business? Here are the steps to open and manage your own membership site:

1. **Your niche market.** It is important to target an audience that is interested about a topic or subject. Find out if your market is big enough before starting a membership site.

2. **Offer something unique.** If you offer the same information that can be found elsewhere on the Internet, then there is no point in launching a membership site. A good strategy is to conduct interviews with experts in your industry, or your own content. That way, you get unique and exclusive content and enjoy credibility for your business.

3. **Look for subscribers.** This step is not as difficult as it seems. Various methods are available for you to use when finding subscribers for your membership site. These

include online newsletters, viral marketing, affiliate programs, pay-per-click, and SEO techniques.

4. **Consider adding special features.** To make it easier for your subscribers to use your membership site, you may opt to add some features such as autoresponder service, credit card processing system, and more.

5. **Enhance your membership site.** Consider adding services, software programs, ebooks, tools, and other resources as giveaways for your subscribers.

Do you have something that you can offer that would be of interest to your market?

Way #15

The Power of Events and Meetups

What better way to reach out to your target customers than meeting them face to face?

Even if you have the best social media marketing campaign in place, it is still not as powerful as the act of interacting with people in person. Yes, communicating with your prospects on the Internet has a potential to spur the growth of your business, but nothing beats face-to-face communication. You can meet your potential customers in person through organizing meetups and events such as product launches, webinars, seminars, workshops, and conferences. Also, you can meet your prospects through online networking services that enable local groups to set up activities outside the Web. These Internet services can help you promote your events to as many people as possible.

One of the best options when it comes to meeting your target customers is to join social media networks such as Google Groups and MeetUp. Within MeetUp, you can find a variety of groups, some of which may match the type of business you have. However, if you cannot find a suitable group, you may also create your own. In addition, you can use this online service to publicize any event that your company regularly holds and target it to the right community.

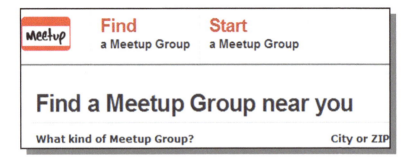

Just like other social media tools, MeetUp enables you to give details about your business to your prospective group members, post photos and other marketing materials, and connect with other members on the message board. It also allows you to organize events online and implement them offline.

Here are the ways to build stronger relationships with your potential customers through events and meetups:

- **Create a mailing list.** Make the most out of your existing groups on your social networks such as a Facebook Group. Use them to keep up conversation among your contacts. An adequate online presence is the first thing you need to be able to attract people into joining the events or meetups you organize.

- **Organize interesting and meaningful meetings.** Make sure that the meetings you host will generate buzz among your members, who will spread the word for you. That is one effective viral or word-of-mouth marketing strategy.

- **Organize various activities.** The purpose of this step is to get the attention of people with diverse preferences and interests.

- **Look for a good location.** Even if your meetup has no budget, it is still possible to hold your meetings or events in a suitable venue such as coffee shops, your office, or someone's home.

- **Listen to feedback.** MeetUp, for instance, allows your member to give ratings of your previous events and make reviews. Learn from the reviews and ratings from your members so that you can improve your future events.

The most important tip is to treat people as humans when you communicate with them online and offline. Even if you spend your entire day interacting with them behind the screen, they want interaction on a personal level with like-minded individuals. Make sure you deliver what your target customers want.

Way #16

Get Viral With Widgets

Have you ever come across those cute little boxes on websites and blogs that you visit? They look cool, right? These boxes are there for good reasons.

Popularly known in the online world as widgets, these mini applications are made up of content that updates dynamically in real-time. They are the smaller versions of some popular social networking sites. Widgets are a fad nowadays. Beyond being a fad, widgets help increase traffic to your website. You can use widgets to enhance your SEO strategies by generating links (with keyword-rich anchor text) to your website. And, as you already know, more traffic means more people visiting your site, which in turn means more online exposure for your business. That being said, it is wise to invest in widgets to complement your social media marketing efforts.

HigherResultsMarketing.com

Small as they may be, widgets are powerful tools in making your website and your brand easily noticed by Internet users.

Widgets are all about interactivity. They allow site visitors to leave short messages to the site owner. The owner of the site, in turn, can reply immediately since widgets are updated in real-time. Widgets also enable you to interact with your site visitors where they are instead of making them approach you. Simply put, widgets make it easy for you to build strong relationships with consumers.

Another benefit of widgets is that these applications do not cost much to create. You can even create widgets for free with the help of some sites.

Are you considering widgets as a part of your social media marketing mix? You have to know first whether using widgets is the right choice. The following are the factors you should look into:

- **Your target audience.** Cool widgets are useless if they have no appeal to your readers. Determine if your audience really wants widgets by performing research on widget directories and social networks such as MySpace and Facebook.

- **The impact of widgets on your business.** Widgets are ideal for building brand awareness, but check if they can be used in conjunction with your other marketing strategies such as RSS feeds or email newsletter.

- **Your available content.** See how much content you can place on widgets. If you lack the content available for widgets, then using these applications may not be worth your effort and time.

- **Promotion of your widget.** Marketing widgets is made possible by widget directories. See if you have the knowledge and abiliy to use the directories that are available online.

- **The extent of help you need for building your widgets.** Especially for complex widgets that require advanced programming skills, you need to have adequate resources for developing your widgets.

Way #17

What Everybody Ought to Know… About Mobile Marketing

Mobile media offers a lot of marketing potential for businesses, considering how very dependent people are to their cell phones and PDAs (personal digital assistants). Most people carry a cell phone with them everywhere they go.

5 Benefits of Using Mobile Marketing in Your Business:

1. Personalized Communication
2. Targeted Marketing
3. Affordable
4. High Response Rates
5. Easily Trackable

If you are thinking about getting started with mobile marketing, you should start by asking yourself who your target market is. Where they live as well as where they get their information (both on the Internet and offline) along with which kind of media they normally use when they are looking to have their needs met are important things to find out. The point is that the more you know about your target market, the greater success you will have with your mobile marketing promotions.

Mobile marketing consists of several different methods of advertising:

Text Messaging/SMS (Short Message Service)

Using mobile phone devices as a marketing tool provides many advantages for businesses. SMS text marketing allows you to reduce your advertising costs while increasing sales and customer loyalty at the same time. This method is inexpensive compared to other marketing methods and usually gets a much higher response rate.

It simply involves sending text messages to consumers promoting a product, service, or brand via a mobile phone. MMS (Multimedia Message Service) is similar to SMS but involves more than simple text messages. It involves more advanced media methods such as sending pictures, video, and audio using mobile devices.

Text messages are sent and received using SMS short codes. An SMS short code is a 5 or 6 digit number, just like a phone number, but shorter and easier to remember.

You need to have a plan to get the permission from your customers to allow your text messages to be received on their cell phones. A common way to do this is to offer something free in exchange for their information. The customer initiates things by texting in a keyword or filling out a form on your website to join your SMS list. In exchange for their subscription, you can offer them an incentive, such as:

- Coupon or discount on your product or service
- Free information that your target audience will find helpful
- Voting / Polling
- Contests/Text2Win

Once the person has subscribed to your text messages, they are now a part of your list and will receive all of your future marketing text messages, which may consist of:

- Free information regarding your product or service
- More coupons and discounts
- Promotional offers
- Event announcements
- Appointment reminders
- Text Message Alerts
    Sports, Weather, Breaking News, Trading Markets
- Text Club
    Exclusive Benefits, Updates, Promos

Cell phone marketing is founded on the concept of choice, which is every marketer's dream. Your customers sign up for your program because they actually want to receive your offers. Marketing just does not get any better than this! In light of the fact that over 90% of text messages are read, you are guaranteed that your customers will see and read what you are offering, and if you come up with a clever marketing strategy, you can offer your customers enticing incentives for following through on your offers. If you take this one step further and offer the recipients an incentive for acting within a specific time frame, you should see an increase in sales immediately.

This is different from marketing in newspapers where you hope the right people will see your ad. Since most people have their cellular devices with them all the time, it only makes sense to offer coupons in a text message. Consumers only have to show the text message at a cash register or give a promotional code when they are paying for a product or service. You can also offer discounts if the offer is acted on in a specified period of time.

If you are suffering from a lack of sales and profits and you would like to take your marketing efforts to a whole new level, then go for it by jumping into the mobile marketing arena. The quicker you jump on board the quicker you can gain a powerful foothold in your specific field of business.

Considering how competitive most fields of business are, as a business owner you must do everything you can to stay in touch with your customers and to offer them services and/or products that they will buy from you.

Keeping in contact with your customer base and offering regular updates regarding your business is a great way to build trust and brand your name.

Mobile marketing that involves sending out promotional vouchers has been proven to be much more effective than the more conventional coupon strategies - six times more effective to be exact.

The Attic, a street wear retail chain in Southern California, using mobile marketing, promoted their sale in only 2 days.

Attic texted 1200 people on their mobile list

Did it work?

232 people showed up before the store even opened (that's 20%)

Attic sold $20,000 in merchandise in a mere 3 hours

Mobile media campaigns are very easy to plan and implement because it only takes a few seconds to send text messages to your target audience. Connecting to your potential customers is also made easy since mobile phones allow them to receive your messages anytime and anywhere. Unlike other marketing tools such as email and blogs, text messages can be easily personalized and are sent to those who have expressed their intent to receive SMS. Since mobile technology can be tapped for viral marketing, mobile marketing is a great complement to your social media marketing campaign. Thanks to Web browser services that modern cell phones have, you can easily forward your messages to your social networks.

Once people have joined, you can use your Facebook or Twitter account to send messages or coupons to the group and to interact with them. Be sure to create an interactive experience with your audience and ask them to respond to you and give you their opinions on your programs, so that you find out what they are looking for that really interests them.

The following are some helpful tips you may consider to get more people interested in what you offer through mobile marketing and to increase awareness of your brand:

- **Personalize your message.** Go to great lengths by getting the first name of your subscriber and using it in your text message. That will make a lot of difference in terms of response rate rather than sending out a generic message to all of your subscribers.

- **Compose your text message in a concise yet clear manner.** Text messages are limited to only 160 characters, so try your best to say everything in the fewest words possible. Using SMS shortcuts (e.g. "2" for "to") is acceptable, but make sure your text message is still readable.

- **Use SMS as a viral marketing tool.** Occasionally, ask your subscribers to invite their friends to subscribe to you if they like your service. Do not forget to include call-to-action statements such as "Text [keyword] to [short code]." You can expect that your network of SMS subscribers will grow over time if you follow this tip.

- **Make sure you send only relevant and timely messages.** People do not want to be interrupted with a lot of SMS all of the time, only to find out that the messages mean nothing to them.

Mobile Websites

More and more people use their cell phone to search for businesses while on the go. But what if your business only has a regular website?

Most mobile devices can't properly display your regular website, making it difficult to locate a simple phone number in most cases. Traditional websites are designed to be viewed on a computer screen instead of a mobile device. This means that most regular websites are not compatible with mobile devices. Depending on the coding of your site, some of them won't even come up at all.

Mobile devices also have small screens, run slower, and have small keypads making it even more difficult to find what they are looking for.

Some websites require endless scrolling sideways and up and down for the user to find even basic information on the page.

If your business offers products or services to consumers, it's in your best interest to make sure they are able to view your website on their mobile devices.

A mobile website makes all of your content easy to read and navigate for all users, which is a MUST if you want to get their business. It makes it easier for "on the go" visitors to easily find your business and contact you with one-click calling, one-click email, and instant directions. This eliminates the need for your customers to take "extra steps" in order to contact or visit your business.

In short, consumers who search their mobile devices for businesses will usually go with those who have a mobile-friendly website. Trying to navigate a regular site on a mobile device is a big headache – just ask any mobile user! It's frustrating.

So, get the edge on your competitors and get a mobile website so mobile users can find you easily. If your potential customers are searching for your type of product or service on their mobile device and come across you and your competitors' websites, they will probably call up the one with a mobile website... simply because they could read it!

QR Codes

QR Codes (Quick Response Codes) - QR codes are two-dimensional bar codes that are used to transfer information through barcode readers that can be found on most mobile devices. Anyone with a camera phone (some may require a bar-code reader) can scan a business's QR code.

QR codes make it easy for Smartphone users to scan codes to get information about your business rather than having to "type" to access your information on their mobile device, or wait until they get home to look at your website.

So, with the snap of a camera phone - or one equipped with a QR code scanner - consumers can scan your QR code and INSTANTLY connect to various forms of digital media or retrieve desired information. A QR code can take them to an opt-in form, a website (preferably a mobile-friendly website), directions to an establishment, a coupon, a video, a menu, picture, a survey, a Facebook Fanpage, Twitter page, and YouTube - the possibilities are endless!

QR codes are helping businesses generate more leads, more sales, and more long-time customers.

Unlike print advertising, QR code content can be quickly and easily changed to promote whatever you want - whenever you want.

7 Ways to Use QR Codes in Your Business

1. Use your QR code on your Google Places Local Business listing page.

2. QR codes can help you build a customer list fast. Create a QR code that links to an opt-in page where consumers will leave their name and email address in exchange for some type of incentive.

3. Integrating social media platforms such as Facebook, Twitter, and YouTube with your mobile website is simple and will help boost your profits even more.

4. Your business's contact information can be instantly stored on their phone.

5. Use your QR code to build a list of mobile subscribers by using mobile keywords and short codes. Using QR codes is the perfect way to make it quick and convenient for your audience to opt-in to your SMS list.

6. QR codes can be easily placed on all of your marketing materials including business cards, T-shirts, flyers, receipts, print advertising, signs, your website, store windows/displays, and many others. If you advertise on billboards or TV, you can put them there too.

7. Use multiple QR codes for different activities and promotions within your business. For instance, if you want to offer a coupon for 10%, create a QR code for it and promote it. If you want to share customer testimonials and reviews, create a QR code for it and promote it. If you want to share information about your newest product that is launching, create a QR code for it and promote it.

There are many other options of what can happen once they scan the code – the choice is yours.

Do you think any of your competitors are currently using QR codes in their business? Probably not... so this is your chance to get a head start on them. If some of them are already using QR codes, this is your chance to keep up with them in your efforts to DOMINATE your market!

Mobile marketing is here to stay. You only have to know yourself, your customers and what it is that you want to accomplish and create a plan for achieving your goals. You will certainly realize that when you get going and have your target audience involved personally, that you will reap the monetary rewards you are after.

Go to www.businessstreamsofincome.com and enter the keyword Mobile or call my office at 1-855-RAINMAKER to see how Mobile Marketing can benefit your business.

Mobile Apps

Mobile Apps (mobile applications) are computer programs that are installed on mobile phones. There are apps that specialize in everything from coupons to finance to locating your favorite restaurant or store.

What does this mean for people who are interested in mobile marketing? By having a mobile app, this puts your business directly at your customers' fingertips. So many people use mobile applications multiple times a day giving you a large group of people access to your company and whatever it may provide.

Mobile apps are so attractive because they offer a more personalized Internet experience. Instead of having to open a web browser and typing in a web address, apps give you access to a site or application of your choice at the touch of a button.

Many larger companies use apps to their advantage by either selling or giving them away. The apps are loaded with either deals or great content to share with the consumers who have installed the apps on their phones.

Your app has to be able to do something that is useful or interesting if your customers are going to want it. Before you make your app, think about what your business can offer through a mobile app to make it valuable to users. You also need to keep your app updated and interactive. If not, your customers will lose interest in your app.

Make sure your app icon is visually appealing and identifiable, because it acts as an extension of your company's brand. Having an app that is attractive, well designed, and has the "cool factor" can draw in potential customers and convince them to learn more about your business and what you offer. When you are considering a design for your app icon and app, consider how the appearance and layout will help to present a positive and appropriate image for your business.

How can your business benefit from mobile apps?

Keep in contact with your customers

Keep them engaged

Keep them coming back

Constant branding

Important information, testimonials, videos, etc

GPS directions to the location

One tap calling

Viral Marketing - "Share This App" - Give incentives to your customers to get others to download your app.

These are a few examples that give users information about your business, all accessible instantly from the user's phone.

What do you think it would do for your sales if you had the ability to send special promotional offers straight to your customers' cell phones?

This is done through "push" notifications. This provides your app with the special capability to send notifications that pop up directly on your customers' phones through your app they downloaded. Instantly, with a push of a button, you can reach the smart phones of thousands of customers. This could mean using your app to share specials, discounts, coupons, reminders, promote special events, daily deals, and more. Ninety-seven percent of people will read these notifications versus four percent with email.

Let's say you are having a slow day. You could send a "push" notification saying "Free_____ for the next hour". Instantly, with the push of a button, you can have more customers coming into your business.

So you can see how having a mobile app not only gives your business one more way to connect with customers as well as reach out to new ones, but also show that your business is keeping up with the latest trends or even leading the way.

The bottom line is that businesses need to reach out to prospects and customers every way they can. If your business doesn't use every communication channel, you are missing valuable opportunities to engage your customers.

No matter where your customers go, they will have their cell phone with them. If your business has a mobile app, you are just a tap away from them at all times.

Chapter 7

Conclusion:
What is Your Social Media Profit Plan?

Social media is one of the best things that ever happened in the Internet. To say that social media has revolutionized the way people do business is an understatement. It has gone beyond that—social media has helped numerous businesses engage and build ties with their current and future customers while giving people the chance to assert their preferences and needs as consumers. Here's the point: Businesses are heading their way to more revenue-generating opportunities, thanks to the power bestowed to them by various social media marketing tools.

This book has given you a walkthrough of 17 social media tools you may need to strengthen the presence of your business on the Web. It is up to you to decide which ones you are going to use. Just make sure that you choose the right tools for your target audience and for the type of business you manage.

To wrap it up, the following are 10 pointers to remember when planning and implementing your social media marketing campaign.

1. Build a strong presence in social media.
2. Monitor your social media presence regularly.
3. Address negative comments about your business promptly, calmly, and professionally.
4. Know which audience to target when planning your social media strategies.
5. Figure out the needs and interests of your target customers.
6. Participate and interact in communities where your target customers belong.
7. Keep your audience engaged. Listen to what they have to say and respond to their comments. Value their feedback too.
8. Provide value to consumers by creating relevant and useful online content instead of a blatant sales pitch.
9. Position yourself and your business as the leader or expert in your industry.
10. Maximize the capability of your social networks to build your brand on the Web.

Ask yourself again: Am I ready to take my business to the next level? After reading this book, you might have a clear idea now of what it takes to make your business attract more customers and generate sales. Social media marketing is what you need to gain a competitive advantage. Be sure, though, that your social media plan is tailor-fit to your needs as well as that of your target customers. That way, you can rest assured that your marketing strategies will work.

FREE
Profit Explosion
Strategy Session
($497 value!)

Here's how to get it:

Contact my office at
1-855-RAINMAKER
and ask for your
Free
Profit Explosion
Strategy Session

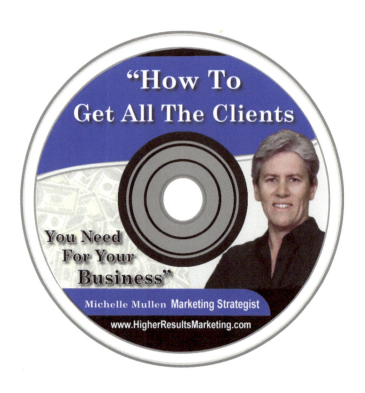

Free CD Offer

Let me send you my CD,

"How to Get All the Clients You Need for Your Business"

All you need to do is get online and go to

www.HigherResultsMarketing.com/freecd

and I will get to you right away!